PLYMOUTH

YESTERDAY TODAY

With Best Wishes
Vic Saundercock.

VIC SAUNDERCOCK

To my wife
Betty

ISBN 0 9510835 1 1

First published December 1989

Published by Vic Saundercock, Eastmoor View, 40 Stephens Road, Liskeard, Cornwall PL14 3SX, UK and printed by Penwell Ltd., Station Road, Kelly Bray, Callington, Cornwall.

INTRODUCTION

There are many books about old Plymouth that brought back memories to the older citizen. I hope my book will bring back more memories, however, I also hope the younger citizen will look at 'Plymouth Yesterday — Today' and identify the present with the past.

A lot of photographs of old Plymouth which you will see, are reproduced by kind permission of Roger Costling of Capetown South Africa and supplied by Ron Andrews of Plymouth, to whom I am grateful.

In addition I thank the following for their help: Brymon Airways, Suzanne Hutchins for her help in the History of Brymon Airways, The Western Morning News, Officers of Plymouth City Police, in particular Mike Newbury, George Webber, Officers of the Devon and Cornwall Constabulary, Jenny Ward, City Reference Library, Officer in Command at the Royal Citadel and many others.

My last book 'Harbour Vessels' was a complete sell out and I was able to donate £800 to the Devon and Cornwall Cavitron Fund. All proceeds (after expenses) from the sale of this book will be donated to the 'First Air Ambulance'—Cornwall Ambulance Service. A little about the Air Ambulance:— To provide a faster and more flexible response to incidents, the UK's first helicopter air ambulance was introduced on the 1st April 1987 as an integral part of the Cornwall Ambulance Service. The air and land ambulances work closely together to provide the best possible service.

A girl climber who fell 30ft onto rocks near Lands End became the first casualty to be air lifted by Cornwall's helicopter ambulance. Miss 18 year old, suffered spinal injuries, resulting from the fall, but within 12 minutes of the pick up, she had travelled to the City Hospital some 30 miles away via the helicopters landing strip at Treliske and by road ambulance. Since that experimental beginning just over 2 years ago some 1,700 missions have been carried out, many lives have been saved. The Air Ambulance survives today because of 'F.A.A.S.T.' First Air Ambulance Service Trust coffee mornings, jumble sales, the 'F.A.A.S.T.' Lottery keep the funds coming. During its first 2 years, the operational costs have averaged £23,000 a month. F.A.A.S.T. needs our help, you might need that helicopter one day.

Vic Saundercock

R. COSTLING

The Head Post Office, Westwell Street, Plymouth.
The Head Post Office, Westwell Street, Plymouth, known as the 'Post Office, Savings Bank, Telegraph, Government Annuity and Money Order Office'. The hours of business for the sale of stamps and Registration of Letters as follows:-

Week Days	8am to 8pm
Sundays	9am to 10.30am

Telegraph Business:- Day and Night
Delivery of parcels etc: 8am to 8pm weekdays
Delivery of letters and parcels: 7am, 11.30am, 2.30pm and 4.45pm, but not on Sundays.

By the clock it is 9.15am, it must be a Sunday morning with only four people about, that soldier is walking smartly across the Guildhall Square, the view you see here, is now Armada Way which you would see across Royal Parade.

In muster at the Old Keyham Gates—later Albert Gate—at Devonport Dockyard. In the bottom right hand corner you can see part of the 'Avondale Arms'. Note the barrow boys selling their wares, with a hackney carriage waiting for a fare.

Today that archway has gone, the clock moved from the other side of the old gate (not shown) the tower building is still there, the large modern building is the covered dry docks known as the frigate complex.

R. COSTLING

The Barbican Fish Market with at least 18 Steam Trawlers tied up. Note the old Victorian Toilets, the fish barrels, the bollards and guard rail and also the steps in the bottom right hand corner.

V.G. SAUNDERCOCK

The Barbican today, same place, the toilets are new, as are the boats tied up there. Note the bollards and guard rail are still there.

R. COSTLING

Coaling Ship, Sutton Harbour, North Quay, a Plymouth steam trawler taking on coal bunkers, a sight not seen today.

V.G. SANDERCOCK

The railway lines, bollards and road are still there, but some of the buildings are new. Stand still and turn right, the next photograph is what you will see there today.

Steam has been replaced by sail, but alas it is not trawlers that use the North Quay any more but weekend sail boats.

V.G. SAUNDERCOCK

Union Street looking towards Stonehouse. The Clock on the building in the foreground is the symbol of W.G. CAPPS, watchmaker and jeweller, No 2 Union Street. In the background the old railway bridge can be seen.

R. COSTLING

The Union Street as we know it today, the roundabout has taken a large part of the top end of Union Street.

V.G. SAUNDERCOCK

R. COSTLING

The New Palace Theatre on one corner of Union Street and E.L. Meadowcroft's big Drapery Shop on the other.

V.G. SAUNDERCOCK

The Palace as we know it today. The Great Western Hotel (the Long Bar to most service men in the past) now gone and replaced by the Malthouse. Meadowcrofts was replaced by a small branch of the Midland Bank, now it is a car show room of Wadham Stringer, the Rover car sales.

R. COSTLING

Inside the old Plymouth Guildhall.

R. COSTLING

Outside the Guildhall a Char-a-banc loaded ready for the outing. Could it be the WI with bottles of cold tea, home made pasty and sticky buns, whoever they are they are going to enjoy the day.

R. COSTLING

The Char-a-banc has gone—there seems to be two ladies who have missed it.

V.G. SAUNDERCOCK

Today the Guildhall still stands, but this side of it is used as a car park.

R. COSTLING

The Lawcourts across from the Guildhall, with the Police Officers on parade, and it looks like the Chief Constable striding out of the entrance with a be-wigged gentleman behind him, this could well be a Judge. As can be seen in the photograph below this is part of the Guilhall Car Park, also the Royal Parade.

V.G. SAUNDERCOCK

The site of the Lawcourts today, now a car park.

V.G. SAUNDERCOCK

St. Andrews Abbey Hall. The workmen are from Pearn Brothers, Building Contractors in the middle of demolishing the old Abbey Stables and Warehouse which had been used as a Bacon Factory and purchased by St Andrews Church in 1921. Note the wooden scaffolding outside the building, each section is tied with rope, although not seen here, the wooden poles were normally stood in barrels for support.

On the 19th September 1923, The Lord Bishop of Bradford (Dr. Perowne) laid the foundation stone for the re-building of Abbey Hall as a 'War Memorial' for those who gave their lives during the 1914 1918 War. The Abbey Hall today was completed in 1926.

R. COSTLING

V.G. SAUNDERCOCK

The foundation stone located in the entrance on the west side of the building.

R. COSTLING

A sad occasion a Royal Naval gun carriage funeral entering St Catherine's Church, Lockyer Street, Plymouth. Beyond the Church is the Lockyer Hotel, across the road is the Royal Hotel and Assembly Rooms. Derry's Clock still stands to remind us of Plymouth yesterday.

V.G. SAUNDERCOCK

Today, the Royal Hotel is a multi storey car park, the Lockyer Hotel and St Catherine's Church are part of the Council car park, but Derry's clock, although lost in the large buildings around it, stands defiant, shift me if you dare.

The Sherwell Congregational Chapel built in 1864, with the Sunday School, in Tavistock Road, Plymouth, showing just one van and bicycle. The fence disappeared when the 1939/45 war came, all metal fences were taken to help the war effort. Just a short walk away is Portland Square, it was there whilst in an underground shelter, during a heavy raid on Plymouth on the night of 21st April 1941, seventy-two people were killed, it was said that some entire families were wiped out, when a very large bomb hit the shelter in which they and others were sheltering.

R. COSTLING

V.G. SAUNDERCOCK

The building still stands, the fence has been replaced, the island has been replaced with a modern island and traffic lights, the tram lines have been replaced with the modern yellow ones, parking on one side of the road only.

R. COSTLING

The Offices of the Western Morning News and Mercury, Western Evening Herald, Western Weekly News, Naval and Military Record and Dockyard Gazette Offices, with the staff outside in Frankfort Street, Plymouth. The Weekly News has pictures of the Prince of Wales and the Duke of Cornwall Light Infantry Memorial in Bodmin.

V.G. SAUNDERCOCK

My photograph shows the Western Morning News and Western Evening Herald Offices in New George Street, Plymouth. The City is on the change yet again, the new pedestrian walk about, has made this photograph, into Plymouth yesterday, already.

His Royal Highness The Duke of Cornwall, Colonel-in-Chief of the Duke of Cornwall's Light Infantry unveiled this Memorial on Thursday 17th July 1924, erected by their comrades in memory of the 255 Officers and 4,027 Other Ranks who gave their lives in the Great War—1914-1918. It is worthy to note that His Royal Highness refused to wear his great coat throughout the whole day—although it was raining hard—because troops were not wearing theirs. Did you know His Royal Highness, Edward Prince of Wales, who became King Edward VIII in 1936, was the only son of a British Monarch to be awarded a gallantry award, the Military Cross.

V.G. SAUNDERCOCK

My photograph taken on Wednesday 28th June 1989 outside of what was the main entrance to the barracks, shows the bronze figure of a soldier in battle order standing on a base of granite, it was said that the soldier's face was especially striking and showed a true Cornish man. The Memorial now commemorates those who fell in both World Wars who were DCLI men.

B.N. SAUNDERCOCK

Taken outside W. Mumford's Garage Ltd, at 39 & 40 St Andrew Street, Plymouth, known as 'The Abbey Garage'. The young lady serving petrol was Miss Betty Munday now Mrs Betty Saundercock, wife of the author.

V.G. SAUNDERCOCK

The Abbey Garage has now gone, replaced with the new Plymouth City Magistrates Court.

R. COSTLING

Troops from the Royal Citadel marching down Lambhy Hill, Plymouth. The Royal Citadel is now the home of the 29 Commando Regiment Royal Artillery. Note the Church in the background, the Church of Holy Trinity and Holy Trinity School.

V.G. SAUNDERCOCK

Today all quiet on the Western Front. Note that the Church of Holy Trinity has now gone and replaced with another building, the Mount Edgcumbe Masonic Hall.

R. COSTLING

North Road Station, Plymouth, waiting on platform 3 are these rather dignified people. Mutley Plain is in the background.

V.G. SAUNDERCOCK

The same platform but this time its the 22-13hrs Royal Mail train with Ted Cook as the driver of 'Fair Rosamund' No. 47618 waiting to pull out. An 'Inter City 125' is approaching platform 4. Note the old GWR seats.

R. COSTLING

Kinross Avenue, off Lady Smith Road, Mount Gould, Plymouth. Note—the farm land in the background, this is Efford.

V.G. SAUNDERCOCK

Kinross Avenue as we know it today, gone are the gas lights replaced with electric lights. More houses, better still, where is that farm land known as Efford?

R. COSTLING

Now we are looking up Kinross Avenue, the old road looks a bit rough, hard on the poor horses who had to haul loads up the hill.

V.G. SAUNDERCOCK

Kinross Avenue as we know it today, apart from the road being made up, with a few changes to the houses, its still the same place.

R. COSTLING

These days have gone now, unloading timber in Millbay Docks. Note Mount Edgcumbe Park in the background.

V.G. SAUNDERCOCK

No timber ships in sight, in fact no ships in the inner basin. It is now being filled in to make way for luxury flats. The top end is the Ferry car park, passengers preparing to embark on the Ferry to cross over to France. With the tunnel across to France, will there be a need for this Ferry service?

R. COSTLING

Three 'Char-a-banc's' of Embankment Tours all set for a day's outing. Taken in Higher Street, Plymouth. The Higher Street Dairy is in the background. Note the shirts on the line.

V.G. SAUNDERCOCK

Today the Dairy has gone, a house now stands where the shirts hung from the clothes line. There are some kerbing and cobble stones left from those days of yesterday.

R. COSTLING

The bottom of Wells Street, Plymouth, Great Western Railway horse and carts loaded with coconuts still in their husk. I believe it is near Christmas, look at the shop behind the second cart, that's a Christmas tree hanging from the window.

V.G. SAUNDERCOCK

Today Well Street has gone, but I did find Well Gardens, a lot of difference between the houses then and now.

R. COSTLING

Ready to roll, a coach and four horses in King Street, Plymouth and the corner of Well Street. The banner on the side of the coach reads 'Welcome to the Hero of the-something-Prince'.

V.G. SAUNDERCOCK

Today the nearest to the above is in the next street up Harwell Street, what Hitler failed to do progress did.

R. COSTLING

Stonehouse Bridge—Halfpenny Gate—Plymouth, looking towards Devonport. Note the 'Toll House' a payment of one half penny per person was demanded. To the right of the Bridge was the timber proving area, and to the left were a number of house-boats, and other boats.

V.G. SAUNDERCOCK

The Bridge today, gone is the Toll House, the tram lines, in fact not many people walk across now its free. Note the sailor in uniform, a sight not often seen these days.

V.G. SAUNDERCOCK

The timber proving area, later the bridge was dammed to hold back the water as an emergency water supply during the 1939/45 war. In recent years it became an infill and is now a sports ground.

R. COSTLING

Another 'Toll House', this time at Edgcumbe Place, Millbridge, Plymouth, the Edgcumbe Hotel on the corner sells bottle Bass Beer.

V.G. SAUNDERCOCK

The toll house has long since been pulled down, and the road has been widened. The Edgcumbe Hotel is now a Courage Public House, mine hosts today are Michael and Helen Smith. Note the Methodist Chapel on the right of the photograph, and see the next one.

ADG

The Methodist Chapel at Hotham Place has been converted into purpose designed offices for the Architects Design Group. The photograph shows the interior of the building which was opened August 1989, by the practice. The practice was created by 4 architects who had trained together at the Plymouth School of Architecture.

R. COSTLING

June 23rd Alexandra Rose Day, taken in Ragland Barracks Devonport, inside the East Gate. The Sergeant is smiling with his rose, but the RSM, is not sure if he should buy one or not. That number plate would be on the high price list these days, let alone the two cars.

V.G. SAUNDERCOCK

Time marches on, the entrance is now a playground. However, stand there with your eyes closed, and you can hear the marching feet, orders still bouncing off the buildings around the barrack square. Present Arms!! Stand still you're like a load of flowers in the wind. Yes, those were the days, we who know, won't ever forget.

V.G. SAUNDERCOCK

How many men marched out through this gate to the Railway Station at Kings Road over the years, better still, how many came through to march on the dreaded parade ground.

R. COSTLING

Not far from Ragland Barracks, in Devonport Park, there is a War Memorial, in memory of those Devonport men who fell during the 1914/18 war. I am not sure who the lady is, however, I understand that the gentleman in his regalia is the Mayor of Devonport, and the Chief Constable of Devonport Police.

The War Memorial today, standing there in its glory. I wonder how many can remember the parades held there over the years.

V.G. SAUNDERCOCK

R. COSTLING

Another sad occasion—this time an Army gun carriage funeral at St Johns Church in Duke Street, Devonport. The pub on the corner of St John Street Ope, later became the 'Duke Street Inn'.

V.G. SAUNDERCOCK

The Same place today with flats on the corner of Duke Street and Monument Street, Devonport, progress speaks for itself.

All has not changed, the Old Chapel—above—still stands, see the story on the next page.

The Old Chapel, Devonport.

At the top of Duke Street and the corner of George Street, Devonport, stood the chapel, the quaint old building was originally built for the Unitarians in the year A.D. 1790. The Congregation of the Chapel decayed in consequence of its being understood that Commissioner Fanshaw intimated that all Dockyardsmen who attended the New Chapel would be discharged as disloyal subjects. The Unitarians were known admirers of the French and as the revolution was in full swing at that time three of the sect were executed for taking part in a riot in Birmingham on the 14th July 1791. In 1801 the Chapel became a place for the sale of Wines and Spirits. The building retains its ecclesiastical character, at the time of this photo a Chaplain still performed certain duties.

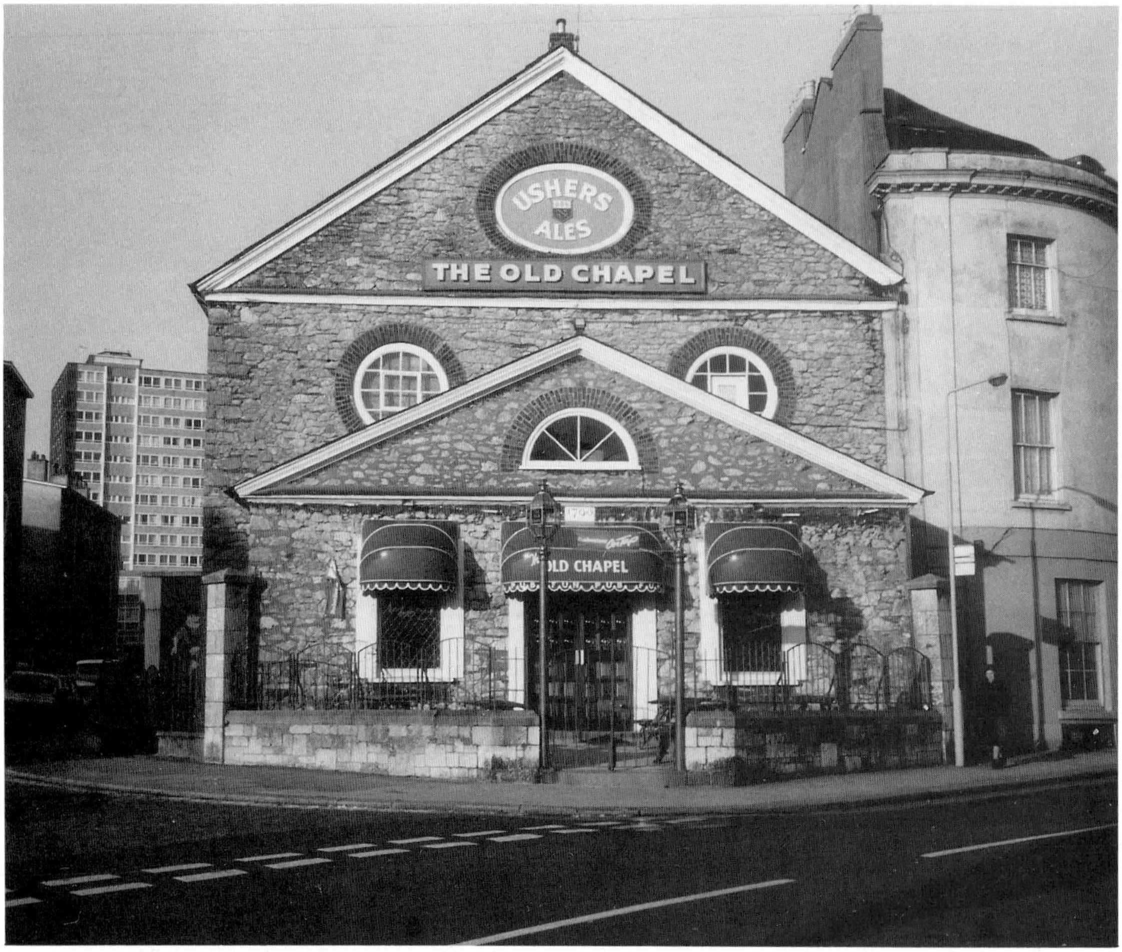

V.G. SAUNDERCOCK

The Old Chapel today, apart from the inside of the Chapel, I remember when I was a child, my Uncle Sid—known as Tich—was the Head Bar and Cellar man in the Chapel then owned by the Barnes brothers, women were not allowed in the bar and it was closed on all religious days, both the inside and the opening hours have changed. I wonder what happened to the Grape Vine that grew outside the front doors.

R. COSTLING

At the junction of Kings Road, Fore Street, Paradise Road, and Trafalgar Place, Devonport, a coach and four horses. Those tram lines can tell a story, a tram came off at this point. Riding that cycle near those tram lines can cause the rider some grief if he got caught up in them.

V.G. SAUNDERCOCK

The same spot many years later, the coach and four have been replaced with a Hopper Bus, the tram lines have gone, replaced with yellow lines.

R. COSTLING

Crossing the Southern Railway Bridge at Paradise Place, Stoke, Devonport, the parade passing the Terminus Hotel. Note all men and boys are wearing hats, the ladies of course wear them at all times.

V.G. SAUNDERCOCK

The bridge today, gone are the tram lines and with them the Southern Railway Station. However, the Terminus Hotel and all the buildings are still there, looking a lot brighter, is it because there are no steam trains, or no trains at all?

R. COSTLING

The United Service Orphan Home for girls, Stoke Terrace, Stoke, Devonport. Where are you today young ladies?

V.G. SAUNDERCOCK

So many years on, during the war our Polish friends used the building as their Naval HQ, but today the department of the Environment use the building as offices. The fire escape has gone, taken for the war effort perhaps.

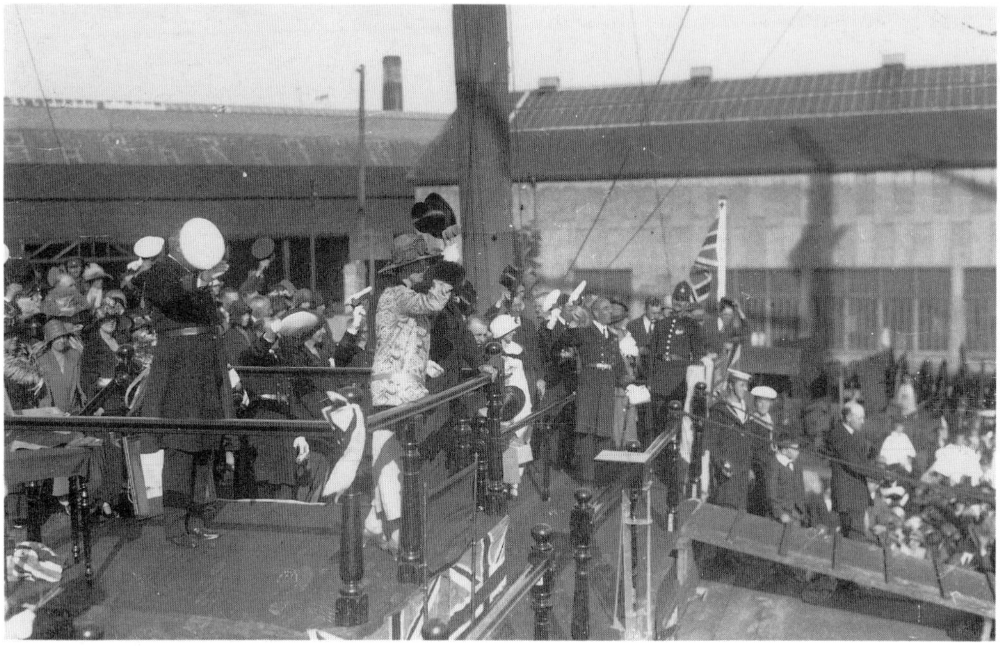

R. COSTLING

There she goes down the slip, South Yard, H.M. Dockyard, Devonport. Many a fine ship has been built on this slip, and many a fine man has built them.

V.G. SAUNDERCOCK

The years have passed, the same slip, but no ship has been built here for many a year. Times have changed, the Dockyard is now a Naval Base managed by a private company, 'DML' Dockyard Management Limited.

R. COSTLING

HMS Royal Oak, passing Rusty Anchor, West Hoe, Plymouth, on leaving the harbour. Some years later on the night of 13/14 October 1939, the German submarine U47*, succeeded in entering Scapa Flow,—where the Royal Oak was at anchor—and fired 3 torpedoes into her, she sank with the loss of 832 crew, including Rear Admiral H.F.C. Blagrove. *(Lt. Commander Günther Prien)

V.G. SAUNDERCOCK

Rusty Anchor today, with no warships to watch sailing in or out, this well known vantage point where people waved their farewells or cheered a ship home over the years, stands empty like Plymouth Sound.

R. COSTLING

The MIGHTY HOOD as she was known throughout the fleet, HMS HOOD passing King Billy at No.1 Slip HM Dockyard, Devonport on her way up harbour. A few years later HMS Hood, whilst engaged in a sea battle with the German Battleship Bismarck at about 6am 24th May 1941, a salvo of 15-inch shells from the Bismarck hit the Hood and in seconds she was gone, blown up with the loss of 95 officers and 1,324 men, there were only 3 survivors. On 27th May 1941 at about 10am after a chase by various HM Ships the Battleships King George V and Rodney blasted the Bismarck with their 14 inch and 16 inch guns, she was soon a blazing wreck and was sent to the bottom by two torpedoes from HMS Dorsetshire. It is understood that there were 115 survivors from Bismarck.

R. COSTLING

HMS Hood under tow from HM Tug Retort as seen from Flag Staff Steps, HM Dockyard, Devonport. A Police Constable from the Metropolitan Police who policed the Dockyard some 50 years ago, watching the Hood come up harbour.

R. COSTLING

All set to go to the regatta, is it the Saltash side or the Devonport side taking part? Note the train going over the bridge, better still note the gasometer, how small it is, but then, where are the houses? better still where are the boats? The next picture might give us a clue.

V.G. SAUNDERCOCK

Same place, no regatta, but look at that gasometer, it has grown, and look at the houses today, and all the boats on the quay. The ferry has gone, but there is another bridge linking the county of Cornwall with Devon.

V.G. SAUNDERCOCK

Today with the rail and road bridges and no ferry, just one man and his wind-surfer. It is hard to believe that prior to June 1944 this area was packed with ships and men waiting for 'D-Day' when they sailed for Normandy.

V.G. SAUNDERCOCK

The Public House is still there and the old ferry boat house is now used by the sea scouts.

R. COSTLING

The old naval training ships in the background, in the foreground is an oil tanker berthed against the old oiling hulk at Wilcove on the Torpoint side of the river.

V.G. SAUNDERCOCK

Today just one modern warship in the background seems to be dwarfed against the floating crane.

V.G. SAUNDERCOCK

The old oiling hulk has gone, that is all thats left of the berth, mind you I understand some good bass have been caught here.

V.G. SAUNDERCOCK

The new oiling jetty, Yondery Pier, with a RFA Tanker alongside, taken from the Lawn at Torpoint, with the tide in, a pleasant spot.

A very old Torpoint Ferry, just landed at Torpoint, the horse and rider trotting ashore, not quite as fast as the motorcycles that come ashore these days.

R. COSTLING

A later model of the Torpoint Ferry, owned by the Cornwall County Council. Again on the Torpoint side, this time she is tied up for the night, a member of the crew coming ashore.

V.G. SAUNDERCOCK

One of the new stretch ferries, looking down the river, from the Torpoint side, note the crew boat.

V.G. SAUNDERCOCK

Another stretch ferry, this time looking up river, with North Yard in the background.

The City Police Forces

Before the Great War—1914-1918—the Police Forces of our city were divided into three, Plymouth, Devonport and Stonehouse, each had its own Chief Constable until the 9th November 1914, when the three Police Forces amalgamated and became Plymouth Constabulary. Some 14 years later the Plymouth Constabulary became Plymouth City Police that was in the year of 1928. In June 1967 Plymouth City, Exeter City, Cornwall and Devon Police Forces amalgamated and became the Devon and Cornwall Constabulary.

DEVON AND CORNWALL CONSTABULARY

The new Plymouth Police HQ at Crownhill, Plymouth, a far cry from the HQ at Westwell Street and at Greenbank Plymouth. The following pages will give the reader an idea of the changes of the Police Force over the years.

R.COSTLING

Detailing officers before going on duty.

R. COSTLING

A big smile before going on duty, or is it off duty?

R. COSTLING

A smart turnout of Police Officers being inspected on the parade ground at the Royal Citadel Plymouth. (All efforts by the author to indentify the inspecting officer failed).

V.G. SAUNDERCOCK

Just a minute, that is not the air ambulance, what can it be?

V.G. SAUNDERCOCK

It's the Royal Helicopter, on the same spot where the Plymouth Police Officers had paraded many years before. Note the same building in the background.

V.G. SAUNDERCOCK

Taken by the author just after Her Royal Highness The Princess Royal had landed at the Royal Citadel.

R. COSTLING

The inspecting officer, inspecting what the author believes are Senior Ranks and CID Officers.

V.G. SAUNDERCOCK

Not Police Officers on parade, but military landrovers lined up on the same spot many years later. The trees are still there, but the guns have been moved away.

V.G. SAUNDERCOCK

A close look at the building today. The bushes are still there and the steps leading up into the building.

R.COSTLING

Sergeants and Officers being inspected, is that a mounted police bike to the right of the photograph?

V.G. SAUNDERCOCK

The same place many years later, an old gun still at the bottom of the steps, the buildings have not changed.

V.G. SAUNDERCOCK

The buildings on the side are still there to this day.

R. COSTLING

Derrys Clock, Plymouth, this was a meeting place for the people of Plymouth. A Plymouth Police Officer on duty there. A part of Derrys Clock can just be seen in the right of the photo.

V.G. SAUNDERCOCK

Gone are the tram lines, however, Derrys Clock still stands in the same place, this photo shows the same part of the clock.

R. COSTLING

Another Police Officer on duty at Derrys Clock junction. Are they all looking at the camera, or the clock?

This is Derrys Clock today, this is what those people would have seen, at 12.20pm.

V.G. SAUNDERCOCK

R. COSTLING

All stop, a Police Officer on point duty. Can it be the Plymouth Sound outside broadcast vehicle. Note the number 12 tram on its way to Fore Street, Devonport.

R. COSTLING

And yet another Police Officer escorting a young charge across the street.

R. COSTLING

A Police wedding at St. Peters Church of England in Wyndam Square, Plymouth. The five men carrying small silver bells must be Police Officers in plain clothes, just look at those boots!

V.G. SAUNDERCOCK

So many years later. The tree is still there, only more mature. The Church is about ⅓ of St. Peters, which was gutted by fire in the blitz, and as can be seen, it now has a flat roof with the top triangle missing.

WESTERN MORNING NEWS

This photograph was taken from the Western Morning News Office, No. 7 Frankfort Street, Plymouth. On the left of the photo you can see L. Cohen's Novelty Stores at No. 40 Frankfort Street, all dressed up for Christmas. In the background you can see W.J. Vickery & Co. Ltd. of 26 & 27 Bedford Street and No. 8 Cornwall Street. The Police Officer on point duty is facing Cornwall Street. Note the Motorcycle Police Officer, in front of Vickery's shop.

WESTERN MORNING NEWS

A regular Constable assisted by a special Constable on crowd control duty during a visit to the city by the Prime Minister, Winston Churchill accompanied by Mrs Churchill, May 1941.

WESTERN MORNING NEWS

The morning after an air raid, the junction of Union Street and Bank of England Place, Plymouth. The bomb damaged shops under the watchful eye of the Constable on duty. Note the Air Raid Wardens in the background.

WESTERN MORNING NEWS

On point duty in Bedford Street, the Constable is facing Goodbody's, tea, coffee specialists, bakers and confectioners (Central Cafe). Next door, Westminster Bank Ltd. In the background the imposing Prudential Buildings which housed the Prudential Assurance Co. Ltd, Restaurant, Viner Carew & Co. Estate Agents, Lloyd, Register of Shipping, The Belgian Consulate and many other offices.

MIKE NEWBURY

Calling all cars, Constable Richard (Dick) Wills on duty in the control room. Note the stolen vehicle list on the wall, no computer in those days, of course there were not many vehicles to be stolen.

I am receiving you HQ. This was a Police car believe it or not. Up to the time of going to print the author has not been able to trace the name of the Sergeant or the driver.

MIKE NEWBURY

D&C CONSTABULARY

Mobile Patrol Sergeant, Alan Trevarthen in a modern Police car, on patrol duty.

MIKE NEWBURY

Oh yes it is a police car, I understand that it had been a Army vehicle taken over by Plymouth City Police and painted black, about 1946. A lot of things to note here, the tyres are odd, the jack is in the front, you can see the traffic indicator under the near side mirror, and of course in those days no seat belts.

D&C CONSTABULARY

Todays Police Car, a Ford Sierra, with Mobile Patrol Sergeant Alan Trevarthen at the wheel.

MIKE NEWBURY

The final parade prior to the amalgamation June 1967. Superintendent Stan Pearce leading the men of the old ''B'' Division down the Royal Parade, Plymouth.

MIKE NEWBURY

The Lord Mayor of Plymouth, Frank Chapman, inspecting the men of ''B'' Division outside the Lord Mayors Parlour.

PLYMOUTH CITY POLICE

1967

The Officers and men of Plymouth City Police taken in this historical photograph with their Chief Constable Ronald Gregory, prior to the amalgamation of Plymouth City Police with the Exeter City, Cornwall Constabulary and Devon Constabulary. (My thanks to George Webber for the loan of this photograph)

V.G. SAUNDERCOCK

Harewood House, Plympton, once the home of the Harewood family, later to become the communal centre for the local people. A fire put paid to the building, and it was closed until a decision for its future could be made.

V.G. SAUNDERCOCK

A decision has now been made, that is to pull down the building and re-build a new Harewood House for the people of Plympton. The old Harewood House has gone, only the trees stand to remind us of the past.

V.G SAUNDERCOCK

The new Harewood House, the trees from the past fit in with the new building, no doubt its a fine looking place, and will be used a lot as a centre for the local people.

V.G. SAUNDERCOCK

The view of Harewood House facing the bowling green, it really blends in with its surroundings.

R. COSTLING

The original 'Hot-cross-bun' shop in the Ridgeway at Plympton. Once the main A38 road with traffic passing through bumper to bumper, not on this day with the street packed with people, still a busy shopping centre.

V.G. SAUNDERCOCK

Harry Stephens Bakers Shop is now a large double fronted building used as a newspaper shop. The National Provincial Savings Bank, now the National Westminster Bank. Gilberts Wines & Spirits etc, is now an Estate Agents Office.

Brymon and the history of Plymouth Airport

On 15th July 1931, His Royal Highness Prince Edward, Prince of Wales, officially declared open Plymouth Airport. If the people of Plymouth thought that commercial aviation had seriously come to the capital of the south west, they were to be sadly disillusioned. In fact, it has taken another 50 years for any real expansion and improvement to be undertaken and whilst, even in the early days, it was recognised that scheduled airline services were a pre – requisite for commercial expansion of Devon and Cornwall, until the 1970's there had never been a viable airline operation. It was not until 1976 that Brymon Airways laid the first tarmac runway.

Those Early Days

In 1919, Plymouth became the terminus of the first ever crossing of the Atlantic by a Curtis Flying Boat of the US Navy. The real story of commercial flying in Plymouth began with an experimental flight in 1923, backed by visionaries of the Chamber of Commerce and the local newspapers, 'The Western Morning News' and 'The Western Independent'. Mail was collected from a transatlantic liner in Plymouth Sound, transferred to an aircraft and then flown up to Croydon Airport, where it was put onto a service to Germany proving that mail from North America could be in Europe within seven hours of arriving by sea this side of the Atlantic. Soon the Ministry of Civil Aviation introduced an experimental service for passengers and parcels between Plymouth, Birmingham, Manchester and Belfast, using open four seater de Havilland bi-planes. In 1923, Roborough was used an an airfield for the first time. By the late 1920's Roborough was a well established flying venue, the site being purchased by the City Council in 1930 for around twenty thousand pounds. In 1933 the Great Western Railway introduced their service from Plymouth toCardiff, in 1935 from Plymouth to Jersey.

The 1930's saw a steady expansion at Roborough with new services, a flying club established, and the opening of a club house.

The second World War put an end to all civil flying activities. After the war various air lines tried to serve Devon and Cornwall, none succeeded.

On 15th June 1972 Brymon Aviation (as it was then called) began its first flight from RAF St. Mawgan (now also Newquay Civil Airport). This was with a nine-seater Britten-Norman BN2 Islander to the Isles of Scilly, just over 30 minutes away.

From that inauspicious beginning at the tiny civil terminal at RAF St. Mawgan, Brymon grew into a scheduled operation. When the airline started in 1972, the company employed only 3 people, apart from senior management. Today the figure is around 300. From 2,500 passengers carried in 1972, the numbers have grown year by year, the number of passengers for 1989 is expected to pass the 100,000 mark for the Plymouth airport.

R. COSTLING

The early freight

Loading parcels of suits from Costers, General Drapers of 3,4,5, and 6, Frankford Street, Plymouth.

V.G. SAUNDERCOCK

Todays freight

Loading a fifty seater DHC Dash Seven aircraft, a lot warmer than the open cockpit of the very early aircraft used from Plymouth.

R. COSTLING

Refuelling with Shell motor spirit at Roborough. Will it get off the ground they seem to be saying. The dog is not worried, he seems to have found a bone buried in the runway.

V.G. SAUNDERCOCK

Passengers leaving a fifty seater DHC Dash Seven aircraft, stepping out onto the tarmac. Note, Brymon laid the first tarmac runway in 1976.

R. COSTLING

Having just arrived climbing down the side of the aircraft, with the open cockpit, you would need a lot of warm clothing on. Note the George Hotel in the background and of course the grass runway.

V.G. SAUNDERCOCK

Leaving the comfort of a Brymon fifty seater DHC Dash Seven.

V.G. SAUNDERCOCK

The George Hotel today, the grass track is still there, but the old aircraft have gone. I understand that the George Hotel is due to go in the future.

V.G. SAUNDERCOCK

No grass track here now but a tarmac runway with a Twin Otter loading passengers for the next flight to Cork in Southern Ireland.

You have seen the photographs, and I have told you of the sinking of the 'Mighty Hood' HMS Hood, and HMS Royal Oak and the terrible loss of life, of course there have been many others. Fifty years ago (1939) with three months of the war behind them, the citizen's of Plymouth were holding a brave face with the loss of the Aircraft Carrier, HMS Courageous and HMS Royal Oak still in their minds. The 13th day of ~~September~~ DECEMBER 1939, became a day to remember, for across the other side of the world, the German pocket battleship Admiral Graff Spee, (Captain Hans Langsdorff) was heading for the River Plate, when she was sighted by the South Atlantic cruiser squadron, HMS Exeter, HMS Achilles and HMS Ajax, Commodor H.H. Harwood was in command of the squadron, which went into action at once. All the British ships suffered damage and casualties.

The Graff Spee was also damaged and Captain Langsdorff decided to make for Montevideo for repairs. The Uruguayan authorities would allow Graff Spee only 72 hours to make repairs. There were many rumours in Montevideo that heavy British ships were now waiting for the Graff Spee to come out, Captain Langsdorff decided to scuttle his ship and on the 17th December 1939 the Graff Spee was sunk in the approaches to the harbour. Captain Langsdorff shot himself on the 20th December 1939.

The news of the battle brought a surge of excitement and pride to Plymouth, more so when the three cruisers returned home to jubilate welcome in Plymouth.

The last moments of a dying ship, the Graff Spee, Montevideo Harbour, 20-54 hrs (8-54pm) Sunday 17th December 1939.

AIRSHOWS IN ACTION

A PRACTICAL GUIDE TO AVIATION PHOTOGRAPHY

First published 1985
Published by Enterprise Aviation Photographs & Publications
42 Claygate Road, London W13 9XG.

ISBN 0 948342 00 5
Printed in Singapore

INTRODUCTION

Aircraft are fascinating subjects and as such are very popular photographic subjects. At first hand, aviation photography may look a difficult subject and only suits those few professionals with their expensive equipment. To photograph aircraft in flight may look a natural thing to do. But before this, there is a number of basic techniques to be acquired in aviation photography.

Action photography not only calls for the use of faster shutter speeds, it also calls for a fast coordination between eye-in-the-finder and finger on the shutter release. Knowing exactly the right moment to release the shutter is largely a matter of education built on previous photographic experience with moving aircraft and a reasonably good knowledge of the subjects themselves. It may take time to get it right but it should become intuitive with practice.

Having first taken aviation photography only a few years ago, I have gone through the whole experience in learning the techniques and then overcoming the technical problems. This book contains a selection of my best action photographs which were taken at air shows around the world. Together with photographic details and useful hints on the various techniques involved in aviation photography.

T.Shia

FRONT COVER	**Mcdonnell Douglas F/A-18A Hornet 161715/XF-25 of VAQ-34 (US Navy)** A spectacular view of a F/A-18A Hornet fighter doing a very fast flypast when the right combination of atmospheric humidity and air speed produced these visible condensation shock waves just as the shutter was released. Note the lesser shock waves above the canopy.	**NAS Point Mugu Open House, USA October 1983** **(Pentax MX 400mm f8 1/1000 Fujicolor HR100)** A very fast shutter speed and the use of a motor drive are essential for this kind of picture. Anticipation and luck are needed as this kind of action is too instantaneous to see and then shoot. The blue Californian skies enhance the quality of the picture considerably.
BACK COVER	**KA-3B Skywarrior, TA-4J Skyhawk, TA-7C Corsair II & A-6E Intruder (US Navy)** This immaculate formation of four different aircraft types from the US Navy, was pictured here doing a slow flypast along the crowd-line. Unusual and varied formations of different aircraft types are not common in air shows in the UK. In general, for photographing	**NAS Point Mugu Open House, USA October 1983** **(Pentax MEF 300mm f11 1/500 Fujicolor HR100)** any formation flypast, a medium zoom lens is the most suitable as the formation may be a tight one or dispersed. Do not forget to use a small aperture to maximize the depth of field in order to ensure all the subjects are in focus.
TITLE PAGE	**Lockheed SR-17A Blackbird 17974 of 9 SRW (USAF)** Silhouetted against the afternoon sky is the unmistakable shape of a SR-71A Blackbird, the world's fastest ever operational aircraft. In plane view, only a few planes have outlines that are sufficiently interesting to justify a shot. This particular SR-71A Blackbird was	**RAF Mildenhall Air Fete '84 June 1984** **(Pentax MX 400mm f5.6+½ 1/1000 Fujicolor HR100)** photographed here performing in its first-ever flying display in Europe. This shot was actually taken outside the airfield where different views of the flying aircraft are possible and sometimes, the light is even more favourable for photography.

CONTENTS

General Dynamics F-16A Fighting Falcon 00612/HR of 50 TFW (USAF)

RAF Fairford Open Day July 1984
(Pentax MX 400mm f5.6+½ 1/1000 Fujicolor HR100)

Pictures of aircraft taking off can be the most dramatic action shots you can have because the dynamic angle of the plane to the ground can inject a feeling of power and movement that is lost in the air. For any take-off or landing shot, try to include the ground in the composition of the picture to serve as a reference level. For fast jets like the F-16, try to use higher shutter speed whenever possible.

Grumman F-14A Tomcat 158625/226 of PMTC (US Navy)

This dramatic action photo shows the F-14A Tomcat carrier-based multi-role fighter climbing steeply away after its take-off run. The F-14A Tomcat is a highly photogenic subject and any picture taken from any angle should look impressive. In addition, the blue skies as a background enhanced the picture considerably.

NAS Point Mugu Open House, USA October 1983
(Pentax MX 400mm f8 1/1000 Fujicolor HR100)

In general, for take-off shots, it is important to select a high shutter speed, to pan the subject movement and if possible to use a motor drive to take a series of successive action shots.

Mcdonnell Douglas F-15C Eagle 00009/BT of 36 TFW (USAF)

A perfect timing is required to capture this shot of a F-15C Eagle showing its upper surfaces as it was doing a barrel roll. The upper surfaces of an aircraft tend to be more interesting to photograph than its underside. Prior knowledge of its flying routine helps one to anticipate its next manoeuvre which should help in getting a perfectly timed shot. The right position of the sun behind the camera is essential in order to brighten up its upper surfaces as it was turning. Note the vapour trails, caused by the reduced pressure in the centre of the swirling vortices of air, streaming away from the wing tips.

RAF Fairford Open Day July 1983
(Pentax MX 400mm f8 1/1000 Fujicolor HR100)

Mcdonnell Douglas F/A-18A Hornet 161705/304 of VFA-113 (US Navy)

NAS Lemoore Photo Day, USA October 1983
(Pentax ME Super 80-200mm f11 1/250 Fujicolor HR100)

This Photo Day was strictly not an air show and it was only for a small group of photographers. There was no special flying display but only routine training and flying activities. It offers a good opportunity to take pictures of local based aircraft, A-7Corsair IIs and F/A-18 Hornets, on a typical normal day. A trip to the edge of the runway resulted in many good action shots of various aircraft doing take-offs, touch and go and landings. A medium zoom lens and a motor drive are the essential equipment to use here.

Mcdonnell Douglas F-4E Phantom 80512/RS & 89464/RS of 86 TFW (USAF)

RAF Mildenhall Air Fete '83 May 1983
(Pentax MEF 300mm f8 1/500 Fujicolor HR100)

These two F-4E Phantoms were doing a formation landing as seen from the landing approach. For landing shots, this location has the advantage that the aircraft are quite low as they cross the airfield boundary. Getting both aircraft without obstructing each other in view is not easy as they always shift position relative to each other. With luck and knowing the right time to release the shutter, it should result in a reasonably good shot. In general, to photograph formation landings or take-offs, a medium zoom lens is the most suitable and not forgetting to use a reasonably good depth of field in order to ensure all the subjects are in focus.

Mcdonnell Douglas F-4E Phantom 66382 of 57 FIS (USAF)

RAF Greenham Common IAT '83 June 1983
(Pentax ME Super 80-200mm f11 1/500 Fujicolor HR 100)

One of the 'star' items at the 25th anniversary F-4 Phantom line-up at the IAT '83 is this 'air superiority grey' camouflaged F-4E Phantom. Luckily, this camouflage scheme on the aircraft shines out on this sunny day. A Phantom aircraft lands and takes off at quite a fast speed so a higher shutter speed is needed to 'freeze' the action on film. The faster the subject goes by, the less time the photographer has to compose his picture, so the more knowledge of the subject he has and together with any previous experience at photographing in similar situations, the better.

Mcdonnell Douglas Phantom FG.1 XT597 of A&EE (RAF)

RAF Greenham Common IAT '83 July 1983
(Pentax MEF 300mm f8 1/500 Fujicolor HR100)

One of the 'star' items in the IAT '83 was this specially painted Phantom FG.1 aircraft from the A&AEE. This photo shows it banking towards the camera as it departs from the airfield. Banking or turning aircraft reveal more of their upper surfaces and are therefore more interesting to photograph. The resulting photo gives an impression of a simulated air-to-air shot of the aircraft. Always use a faster shutter speed for take-offs than for landings in order to avoid unnecessary blurred pictures.

Northrop NF-5A Freedom Fighter K-3021 of 314 Sqn. (RNAF)

RAF Greenham Common IAT '83 July 1983
(Pentax MX 400mm f5.6+½ 1/1000 Fujicolor HR100)

A specially painted red, white and blue NF-5A Freedom Fighter of the Royal Netherlands Air Force, is the official display aircraft designated for participation in air shows throughout Europe. During rehearsals, it was doing a knife-edge flypast when its overall colour scheme can be clearly seen. Always be alert for any surprise manoeuvre especially by small, fast jet aircraft during their flying demonstration. Many spectacular shots have been missed by photographers who were not expecting anything spectacular and were not ready with their cameras.

British Aerospace (BAC) Lightning F.3 XP753 of LTF (RAF)

RAF Wethersfield Air Pageant July 1983
(Pentax MX 400mm f8 1/1000 Fujicolor HR100)

Always a favourite in any flying display, a RAF Lightning F.3 interceptor in its new grey paint scheme, can be seen doing a very fast flypast. So fast that even shock waves appeared on top of its canopy. To photograph any aircraft at such a fast speed, you need the highest shutter speed possible and to follow the subject movement accurately or else you may end up with a half or three-quarters view of an aircraft in the picture. If you are lucky, you may capture any resulting shock waves or condensation vapours on film.

British Aerospace (BAC) Lightning T.5 XS459/DW of LTF (RAF)

RAF Finningley Battle of Britain 'At Home' Day September 1984 (Pentax MX 400mm f8 1/1000 Fujicolor HR100)

This grey and green camouflaged Lightning T.5, a two-seater trainer version of the Lightning all-weather interceptor, will be replaced soon by the Tornado F.2 aircraft. Seen here doing a tight turn as it comes over to land at RAF Finningley to be displayed in the static park. Note the landing flaps and airbrakes are fully deployed. When photographing from the ground, there is this persistant problem of extreme contrast between the dark underside of the aircraft and the bright sky.

British Aerospace Sea Harrier FRS.1 XZ458/H124 of 800 Sqn. (RN)

RAF Mildenhall Air Fete '81 May 1981
(Pentax MX 400mm f8+½ 1/500 Kodacolor II)

This RN Sea Harrier FRS.1 multi-role combat aircraft with its rather bright colour scheme, was photographed before the Falklands conflict. This long telephoto lens view was taken at the end of the runway as the aircraft was quite low as it came 'over the fence'. For photography at the landing approach, the distance between the landing aircraft and the photographer standing more or less in the same location, is almost constant. This should help him to assess the likely distance apart and then choose the appropriate lens to use for any incoming aircraft.

British Aerospace Sea Harrier FRS.1 ZA195/710 of 899 Sqn. (RN)

A fully armed Sea Harrier FRS.1 aircraft climbing up steeply and departing from Farnborough after participating in the air show. The four Sidewinder AAMs are clearly visible from this viewpoint. Its new dark grey paint scheme with black letters and markings, almost matches the grey overcast skies above the airfield.

Farnborough International Air Show '84 September 1984
(Pentax MX 400mm f8 1/500 Fujicolor HR100)

The departure day itself provides an excellent opportunity to photograph most of the aircraft, both static and flying participants, in action as they depart from the airfield. Sometimes, they may carry a full weapon load and auxiliary fuel tanks.

Panavia Tornado F.2 ZD 901 (RAF)

A dramatic view of a Tornado F.2 interceptor rolling down the runway in its take-off run. Its powerful engines created a shimmering haze over the whole background, right behind the rolling aircraft. This impressive head-on shot of an aircraft taking off is not the usual side-on or three-quarters view you see in most take-off photos. Unless you are very near the runway, you need a long telephoto lens for this kind of shot.

Farnborough International Air Show '84 September 1984
(Pentax MX 400mm f8 1/500 Fujicolor HR100)

Panavia Tornado F.2 ZD 901 (RAF)

Farnborough International Air Show '84 September 1984
(Pentax ME Super 80-200mm f8+ ½ 1/250 Fujicolor HR100)

On a dull and wet day, this Tornado F.2 interceptor can be seen climbing away with its afterburners fully lit up and clearly visible against a dark background. This spectacular take-off shot was taken using accurate panning technique and choosing a suitable background as a backdrop. A good location for this kind of shot is the mid-point along the runway which is usually the lift-off point for most aircraft. It so happened that at this location at Farnborough airfield, trees form a wooded, undistracting background.

Dassault-Breguet Mirage F.1EJ No.112 of 1 Sqn. (RJAF)

RAF Greenham Common IAT '83 July 1983
(Pentax ME Super 80-200mm f11 1/250 Fujicolor HR100)

This brand new Royal Jordanian Air Force's Mirage F.1EJ fighter aircraft with its three-tone camouflage scheme of brown, sand and green, is one of three similar aircraft that took part in the IAT '83. It was making its only ever appearance in the UK. A unique and rare chance to photograph it for one's collection. This side-on and at tree-top level view of the aircraft which was about to land, has the advantage that it was quite low as it crossed the airfield boundary. Its twin ventral airbrakes are fully deployed.

Dassault-Breguet Mirage 2000-02 (Fr.AF)

In this photo of a prototype Mirage 2000 fighter aircraft about to land at Farnborough's runway, the background and foreground are actually being emphasized and made to provide an 'air show atmosphere' to the picture. It also shows well the compression of perspective which is the hallmark of a 400mm telephoto lens. As in any action shot, it illustrates the importance of selecting a high shutter speed, panning the subject movement and pre-focussing on the point at which the shutter will be released.

Farnborough International Air Show '80 September 1980
(Pentax MX 400mm f11 1/500 Kodacolor II)

Fairchild-Republic A-10A Thunderbolt II 00280/WR of 81 TFW (USAF)

RAF Wethersfield Air Pageant July 1983
(Pentax MX 400mm f8 1/1000 Fujicolor HR100)

A regular participant at many flying displays in the UK is this A-10A Thunderbolt II close-support attack aircraft which are based in RAF Bentwaters and RAF Woodbridge. This perfectly timed shot captures the aircraft as it was doing a barrel roll and it also shows its wing flaps being deployed in both direction. There is ample opportunity for this kind of picture when the aircraft is doing a knife-edge flypast, turning steeply to land or doing a barrel roll.

General Dynamics F-111E 70115/ED of AFFTC (USAF)

Edwards AFB Open House, USA October 1983
(Pentax MX 400mm f8 1/1000 Fujicolor HR100)

Without any prior announcement, this F-111E attack aircraft was disposing its excess fuel and burning it with its afterburners. Today, this kind of spectacular demonstration of the 'hot pass' is very rare at air shows, even the Royal Australian Air Force's F-111Cs have been banned from doing this stunt. Note the vortices streaming away from its wings and fuselage of this tight turning F-111E. During any flying display, always be alert for surprises as many spectacular shots have been missed by photographers who were not expecting anything special and were not ready with their cameras.

General Dynamics F-111E 80077/UH & 80078/UH of 20 TFW (USAF)

RAF Upper Heyford Open Day August 1983
(Pentax MX 400mm f8 1/1000 Fujicolor HR100)

The immaculate formation flypast by these two F-111Es with gear down and their wings fully extended, was pictured against a perfect blue sky which is not very common in the UK. This sharp picture also shows clearly its span-wise flaps being fully deployed. In general, for any formation flypast, a medium zoom lens will be the most suitable but in this case as the formation is quite high up, so a 400mm telephoto lens was used instead.

Grumman A-6E Intruder 155703/AG 505 of VA-65 (US Navy)

RAF Mildenhall Air Fete '83 May 1983
(Pentax MX 400mm f8 1/1000 Fujicolor HR100)

Usually the day after the air show is the departure day for most if not all the aircraft that took part in the air show. Morning is usually the busiest time for aircraft departures. A good opportunity to take action shots of aircraft that were displayed statically. Sometimes, some of these departing aircraft may do one or two farewell flypasts over the airfield, just exactly what this A-6E Intruder was doing. For photographing any flypast by small, fast aircraft, a 400mm telephoto lens is the most suitable as it can be comfortably hand-held.

Mcdonnell Douglas TA-4J Skyhawk 153676/711 of VA-127 (US Navy)

This two-seater trainer version of the A-4 Skyhawk ground attack aircraft is pictured here rolling down the runway in its take-off run. The TA-4J Skyhawk is not only used for advanced pilot training but also for dissimilar aircraft combat training in the US Navy. From the near edge of the runway, this beautiful action shot was taken by using a medium fast shutter speed and panning the subject movement which resulted in a sharp image of the aircraft set against a blurred, undistracting background.

NAS Lemoore Photo Day, USA October 1983
(Pentax ME Super 80-200mm f11+½ 1/250 Fujicolor HR100)

Vought A-7E Corsair II 1605411/311 of VA-22 'NH' (US Navy)

NAS Lemoore Photo Day, USA October 1983
(Pentax ME Super 80-200mm f11+½ 1/250 Fujicolor HR100)

This beautiful shot of an A-7E Corsair II attack aircraft doing a touch and go, was taken by using a medium fast shutter speed and panning the camera accurately. A successful panning technique is the key to good action photos. This well-panned shot gives the impression of movement, with a sharp subject and a blurred background. The light which is behind the photographer, is perfect as it should be.

Vought A-7E Corsair II 160710/710 of NWC (US Navy)

NAS China Lake Open House, USA November 1983
(Pentax MX 400mm f8 1/1000 Fujicolor HR100)

The setting is purely scenic with the spectacular mountains behind this A-7E Corsair II attack aircraft as it was taxiing back to its flightline after completing its flying demonstration. Its new low-visibility colour scheme blends well with the background, so you may say it is a perfect camouflage after all. An aircraft with its wings folded and its canopy raised should make a more interesting picture. Getting good taxiing shots is often the case of knowing in advance the right spot to be at and also bearing in mind the direction of light falling on the subject.

British Aerospace Harrier GR.3 XZ964/P of 233 OCU (RAF)

RAF Brize Norton Open Day June 1983
(Pentax MX 400mm f8 1/1000 Fujicolor HR100)

A classic photo of a RAF Harrier GR.3 tactical attack aircraft in a very fast flypast, showing condensation vapours shimmering above its wings as it pulls round in a very tight turn above the airfield. Note the shock waves above its engine intakes. To illustrate these shock wave effects clearly, it is necessary to use a very fast shutter speed to 'freeze' the action. It is impossible to take this kind of shot without some good luck and being always alert during the flying display. This photo was actually taken outside the airfield where on this location the light on the subject was more favourable.

British Aerospace Harrier GR.3 XV738/B of 233 OCU (RAF)

RAF Finningley Battle of Britain 'At Home' Day September 1984 (Pentax MX 400mm f8 1/1000 Fujicolor HR100)

Making its public debut in the new grey low-visibility colour scheme is this Harrier GR.3 attack aircraft, shown here on finals for its attendance at the air show. When this photo was taken, the sun was towards one end of the runway, so the light on the subject was not relatively uniform. Another problem is the extreme contrast between the dark underside of the aircraft and the bright blue sky. A skylight filter can be used to reduce the excessive bluishness that often occurs when taking pictures under a bright blue sky. This filter also serves as a permanent protective cover on the lens against dust or scratches.

Panavia Tornado GR.1 ZA598 of TWCU (RAF)

RAF Alconbury Air Tatoo July 1984
(Pentax MX 400mm f8 1/1000 Fujicolor HR100)

A frequent participant in both static and flying displays is the Tornado GR.1 multi-role combat aircraft, one of which is seen here cleaning up after a touch and go flypast. The sharp image of the aircraft and the blurred background help to convey an impression of fast motion which this aircraft is fully capable of. A long telephoto lens of 300mm or 400mm is the most suitable for photographing small, fast jet aircraft in action.

SEPECAT Jaguar GR.1 XX754/23 & XX766/14 of 226 OCU (RAF)

RAF Upper Heyford Open Day August 1983
(Pentax ME Super 80-200mm f11 1/250 Fujicolor HR100)

This view of two Jaguar GR.1 attack aircraft on the landing approach, shows they are well spaced apart from each other. A Jaguar aircraft by itself is not a photogenic subject at all but a pair of them in formation flight makes a more interesting picture. For photographing a formation of aircraft and not knowing in advance how far apart they will be from each other, the best lens to use is a medium zoom with its variable focal lengths. To keep both far and near subjects in focus, a good depth of field is essential too.

Dassaut -Breguet Mirage VBD BD-03 of 8 Sqn. (Bel. AF)

Rarely seen in any flying display is this Mirage VBD, a two-seater operational trainer version of the Mirage V fighter-bomber. Its dual role is ground attack as well as training. It was photographed here flying over the airfield to signal its arrival. As it was a very fast flypast, you need to use a fast shutter speed to 'freeze' the subject movement and to pan the camera to follow its movement in flight. The faster the subject goes by, the less time the photographer has to compose his picture.

RAF Finningley Battle of Britain 'At Home' Day September 1984
(Pentax MX 400mm f8 1/1000 Fujicolor HR100)

Boeing B-52H Stratofortress 00057/5D-C of 410 BW (USAF)

RAF Greenham Common IAT '81 July 1981
(Pentax ME Super 80-200mm f11+½ 1/250 Kodacolor II)

One of the most photogenic aircraft is the B-52H Stratofortress heavy bomber, one is seen here heading skywards after the IAT '81. Flying demonstration by any B-52 is very rare in the UK where it is more commonly seen as a static exhibit or during its regular deployments here from the US. This three-quarters rear view shows the wheels are in the half-way up position and the 'invasion-type' markings on its wings and lower fuselage. Some aircraft types look better and more interesting from certain angles. For example, in this picture, the B-52H Stratofortress looks more impressive with its long wings and eight engines visible.

Rockwell International B-1A 760174 (USAF)

Farnborough International Air Show '82 September 1982
(Pentax ME Super 80-200mm f11+½ 1/250 Fujicolor HR100)

On a certain Thursday, the arrival of the B-1A strategic bomber to participate in the Farnborough IAS '82, was eagerly awaited by a huge crowd of photographers, aircraft enthusiasts and the whole media too, on both inside and outside the airfield. There was intense excitement in the air when it finally appeared over the skies above Farnborough. Photographers were running everywhere to find the right spot to take some good action shots. Farnborough airfield is not the best place for taking landing shots as there are buildings, chimneys and trees everywhere around the landing approach area.

Rockwell International B-1A 760174 (USAF)

Farnborough International Air Show '82 September 1982 (Pentax MX 400mm f8 1/1000 Fujicolor HR100)

After making its first overseas visit, this desert camouflaged B-1A strategic bomber is pictured here departing for home after attending the air show. To the surprise of the waiting photographers, it did a slow farewell flypast over the airfield. A rare opportunity to take some good action shots of a B-1A set against a rarely seen blue sky over Farnborough. This early morning shot was taken with a 400mm telephoto lens fitted with a skylight filter which helps to reduce the excessive bluishness that frequently occurs in outdoor colour photography especially under a clear blue sky. Note the swirling vortices of air streaming away from above its wings.

British Aerospace (EE) Canberrra B.2 99+35 of Est. 61 (WGAF)

RAF Greenham Common IAT '83 July 1983
(Pentax ME Super 80-200mm f11 1/250 Fujicolor HR100)

One of the 'star' items in the static park is this orange-coloured Canberra B.2 aircraft, one of only 2 or 3 serving with the experimental unit Erprobungstelle 61 (Est.61) of the West German Air Force. This aircraft is rarely seen at air shows in the UK and whenever it appeared, it usually attracted a lot of attention from the crowds. To the delight of the waiting photographers, this aircraft obliged with one or two flypasts before landing at the airfield.

British Aerospace (Avro) Vulcan B.2 XM597 of 50 Sqn. (RAF)

A long telephoto lens was used to take this simulated air-to-air shot of a Vulcan bomber banking towards the airfield for a flypast. Any flying display by a Vulcan bomber is always very popular with the crowds. But sadly at present, the Vulcan have disappeared from RAF service except for one or two aircraft temporarily kept for display in a limited number of air shows around the UK. The subject matter was enlarged considerably to fill up the picture as it managed to fill up only half the negative. A 600mm or 800mm telephoto lens would be more suitable or even adding a teleconverter to a 400mm lens.

RAF Brize Norton Open Day June 1983
(Pentax MX 400mm f8 1/1000 Fujicolor HR100)

British Aerospace (Avro) Vulcan B.2 XL426 of 50 Sqn. (RAF)

RAF Mildenhall Air Fete '83 May 1983
(Pentax ME Super 80-200mm f11 1/250 Fujicolor HR100)

Occasionally on landing, the Vulcan bomber aircraft will deploy its huge brake chute to slow down its landing run. Although it was a wet and dull day, this particular shot offers better details because the shadows are much softer. Using a medium telephoto or a medium zoom lens and positioning yourself around the half-way point along the runway, it should not be difficult to get a similar shot. When photographing along the runway, beware of foreground obstacles like the standing policemen, runway markers or PA pylons.

Boeing NKC-135A Stratotanker 53135/ED of AFFTC (USAF)

Edwards AFB Open House, USA October 1983
(Pentax MX 400mm f8 1/1000 Fujicolor HR100)

One of the most interesting items in the flying display at this Open House is this unique formation which consists of a NKC-135A Stratotanker refuelling an A-37B Dragonfly with an attending shark-mouthed YF-4E Phantom waiting for its turn. A big disadvantage in photographing the flying display at Edwards AFB is that most aircraft were flying well away from the crowd-line. A 400mm telephoto lens is only barely adequate for photographing this formation flypast. Note the reflected light from the desert surroundings helps to brighten up the underside of these aircraft.

Douglas KA-3B Skywarrior 138944/GD-220 of VAQ-34 (US Navy)

NAS Point Mugu Open House, USA October 1983
(Pentax MEF 300mm f11 1/500 Fujicolor HR100)

Air-refuelling demonstrations like this one involving a KA-3B Skywarrior and an A-6E Intruder, are more frequent in air shows in the US. This photo shows an actual 'hook-up' demonstration whereas in the UK, more often than not, it usually involved a simulated link-up. In this demonstration, the aircraft involved have to do a very slow flypast. So by using a medium fast shutter speed and with the help of a motor drive, it should not be difficult for any photographer to obtain a series of good action shots.

Lockheed C-5A Galaxy 80222 of 436 MAW (USAF)

The 'star' item in the flying display is the appearance of a C-5A Galaxy, the world's largest transport aircraft. It did two slow flypasts, one with gear down and the other in the clean configuration. As it flies in slowly along the crowdline, there is ample time to take a few good flying shots of this aircraft. In general, a medium zoom lens is the most suitable for photographing flypasts by big aircraft like this C-5A Galaxy.

RAF Upper Heyford Open Day August 1983
(Pentax ME Super 80-200mm f16 1/250 Fujicolor HR100)

Lockheed Hercules W.2 XV208 of RAE

RAF Fairford Open Day July 1984
(Pentax MX 400mm f8 1/1000 Fujicolor HR100)

A weather meteorological version of the hugely successful C-130 Hercules family, is this Royal Aircraft Establishment's Hercules W.2 aircraft, pictured here in action doing a knife-edge flypast. As it is nearing the end of its service life, it was a frequent participant at many air shows around the UK throughout 1984. This long telephoto lens view shows clearly its upper surfaces and the meteorological radome above the cockpit.

Mcdonnell Douglas KC-10A Extender 91713 of 2 BW (USAF)

RAF Greenham Common IAT '83 July 1983
(Pentax ME Super 80-200mm f11+½ 1/250 Fujicolor HR100)

On the main arrival day, this KC-10A Extender tanker and transport aircraft, one of hundreds of aircraft of all types and from all over the world, can be seen coming here to participate in the IAT '83. It was a field day for photographers and aircraft spotters, that is if they can find a good spot to stand on. An advantage in getting good landing shots compared to take-off shots is that the aircraft are usually going much slower and are at a much more constant altitude as they come 'over the fence'.

British Aerospace 146 ZD696 of 10 Sqn. (RAF)

RAF Brize Norton Open Day June 1983
(Pentax MX 400mm f8 1/1000 Fujicolor HR100)

This BAe 146 passenger transport aircraft is one of only two in service with the RAF. Seen here making its public debut at its home base. This photo was actually taken outside the airfield at the spot where flying display aircraft usually bank steeply before landing. Moreover, the light was more favourable here than on the crowd-line inside the airfield. Even with a 400mm telephoto lens it still doesn't fill up the whole frame. Therefore, you really need a lens of longer focal length for this kind of shot. The blue sky enhances the picture considerably as the subject is basically in white colour scheme.

British Aerospace (HP) Victor K.2 XH671 of 55 Sqn. (RAF)

RAF St. Mawgan International Air Day August 1984
(Pentax ME Super 80-200mm f11+½ 1/250 Fujicolor HR100)

On the arrival day, this 'hemp' camouflaged Victor K.2 tanker aircraft is pictured here just about to touch-down. There are certain situations in both landings and take-offs that can add more interest to the picture, if caught at just the right moment. As in this photo, the landing wheels are just inches or only a few feet away from touching down. This touch-down point is the ideal spot for good landing shots. Another good reason is that the reflected light from the runway tarmac helps to brighten up the lower fuselage and the wings so that the light on the subject is relatively uniform throughout.

Yakovlev Yak-40 'Codling' 71504 (Yugo.AF)

Farnborough International Air Show '84 September 1984
(Pentax MX 400mm f5.6 1/1000 Fujicolor HR100)

This rarely seen Yakovlev Yak-40 passenger transport aircraft of the Yugoslavian Air Force was photographed on the day after the air show. Having arrived in the morning, it was then parked well away in a secluded part of the airfield. With the help of a 400mm telephoto lens and literally photographing through the wire meshes of the boundary fence, I still managed to fill only half the frame. This shows clearly how far away it was parked from the fence. For photographing through wire meshes, you need to use the widest aperture possible to ensure a sharp subject and blurred background and foreground.

Lockheed CP-140 Aurora 140111 of 415 Sqn. (Can.AF)

A CP-140 Aurora ASW aircraft, a Canadian AF's version of the P-3 Orion, seen here on finals for its attendance at the air show. As the photo was taken in very sunny conditions, the problem of extreme contrast between the dark underside of the aircraft and the bright blue sky is clearly illustrated. As a result, sunny conditions may not provide the ideal lighting on the subject after all. Whereas, overcast conditions may offer better details because the shadows are much softer or completely absent. But on the other hand, any flying aircraft set against a dull overcast sky does not look as attractive as when it was taken against a blue sky.

RAF Greenham Common IAT '83 July 1983
(Pentax ME Super 80-200mm f11+½ 1/250 Fujicolor HR100)

Dassault-Breguet Alize No.56 of 4F Aeronavale (Fr. Navy)

RAF Greenham Common IAT '83 July 1983
(Pentax MEF 300mm f11 1/500 Fujicolor HR100)

A side-on view of an Alize Aeronavale's shipboard ASW aircraft, seen here arriving for the IAT '83. With its slower landing speed, a slow shutter speed can be used which also helps to prevent its propellers from being 'frozen' still. Another common problem in aviation photography is the occurrence of glaze from the aircraft's canopy in very sunny conditions. Unwanted reflections can be reduced or removed by fitting a polarizing filter to the lens but its main drawback is that you have to stop-down the aperture by 2 f-stops. Choosing a slightly different camera angle may help to remove the problem too.

Dassault-Breguet Atlantic No.31 of 23F Aeronavale (Fr.Navy)

This striking head-on view of an Atlantic ASW aircraft of the Aeronavale, seen here on its landing approach to RNAS Yeovilton to participate in the air show. Its surveillance aerials and leading edges are clearly visible from this viewpoint. By experimenting with different camera viewpoints, you will notice that some aircraft types look better or more interesting from certain angles than others.

RNAS Yeovilton International Air Day August 1984
(Pentax MX 400mm f8 1/1000 Fujicolor HR100)

Dassault-Breguet Atlantic 61+13 of MFG.3 (Ger. Navy)

RAF Greenham Common IAT '83 July 1983
(Pentax MEF 300mm f11 1/500 Fujicolor HR100)

Normally, the underside of an aircraft does not make an attractive photo. But sometimes, the views from below are good for showing details not noticeable from other angles. In this case of an Atlantic ASW aircraft flying directly overhead the camera, the contents in the opened weapons bay can be seen clearly. This shot was actually taken outside the airfield as most aircraft in the flying display are not permitted to fly directly over the crowds. Unfortunately, a few minutes later, this aircraft burst its main tyres on landing and caused a runway obstruction for a while.

Boeing E-3A Sentry 50557 of 552 AW&CW (USAF)

RAF Mildenhall Air Fete '82 May 1982
(Pentax ME Super 80-200mm f16 1/250 Kodacolor II)

Although more commonly seen as a static exhibit than in the flying display, this E-3A Sentry airborne warning and control system (AWACS) aircraft was seen here heading skywards on the departure day. This departure day provides an excellent opportunity to take some good action shots of most if not all the aircraft that participated in the air show. A medium zoom is the most suitable lens to use for take-off shots of larger aircraft whereas a 400mm telephoto for smaller aircraft.

Grumman E-2C Hawkeye 160988/NH-603 of VAW-117 (US Navy)

NAS Point Mugu Open House, USA October 1983
(Pentax MEF 35-105mm f16 1/250 Fujicolor HR100)

The US Navy carrier-borne AEW aircraft is this E-2C Hawkeye, pictured here in the static park. For photography of the static display in most air shows, a major disadvantage is that many interesting aircraft are flanked by viewing ramps, support equipment, signboards and barrier fences or ropes. To get an uncluttered view, you need a little patience as onlookers tend to congregate around the static aircraft. Another good advice, always try to get to the air show early in the morning before the crowd arrives and you may be able to get some good clean static shots.

Lockheed EP-3E Orion 150494/JQ 25 of VQ-2 (US Navy)

RAF Wyton Open Day July 1984
(Pentax MEF 35-105mm f11 1/250 Fujicolor HR100)

This EP-3E aircraft is an electronic intelligence gathering version of the P-3 Orion which features some systems modifications, for example, addition of the dorsal and ventral radomes which can be clearly seen in this picture. In this static shot, having a car park as a background is undesirable as it looks like an unnatural setting. By using a large aperture it is possible to blur out partly the undesirable background so as to be not so intrusive to the main subject.

McDonnell Douglas F-4G Wild Weasel 97202/SP of 52 TFW (USAF)

A variant of the F-4 Phantom family is this F-4G Wild Weasel electronic warfare aircraft, seen here carrying an AGM-65 Maverick missile on its starboard inboard pylon. This three-quarters rear view of the aircraft set against a blurred background, adds to the atmosphere of the picture by creating the impression of speed. This action shot clearly illustrates the importance of selecting a high shutter speed, panning the subject movement and pre-focussing on the point at which the shutter will be released.

RNAS Yeovilton International Air Day August 1982
(Pentax ME Super 80-200mm f11+½ 1/250 Kodacolor II)

British Aerospace (HS) Shackleton AEW.2 WL790/90 of 8 Sqn. (RAF)

RAF Wyton Open Day July 1983
(Pentax ME Super 80-200mm f16 1/250 Fujicolor HR100)

Nearing the end of its service life is this Shackleton AEW.2 aircraft photographed here in action over RAF Wyton. Although still awaiting to be replaced by the Nimrod AEW.3, its participation in flying displays is getting rarer each year, so therefore, it may be the last chance to photograph it for one's collection before it disappears forever.

British Aerospace (HS) Nimrod AEW.3 XZ286 (RAF)

Farnborough International Air Show '80 September 1980
(Pentax MX 400mm f8+½ 1/500 Kodacolor II)

The long-awaited replacement for the veteran Shackleton AEW.2 aircraft is this Nimrod AEW.3, the first development aircraft is seen here in action over Farnborough. It began its flying display with this knife-edge flypast. This view of the aircraft was taken with a 400mm telephoto lens which only just managed to fill the whole frame. As such, it clearly illustrates the usefulness of such a lens at flying displays as most aircraft do their flying demonstration well away from the crowd-line as a public safety measure.

Lockheed SR-71A Blackbird 17980 of 9 SRW (USAF)

RAF Greenham Common IAT '83 July 1983
(Pentax ME Super 80-200mm f8+½ 1/500 Fujicolor HR100)

The 'star' item in the static park is this SR-71A Blackbird strategic reconnaissance aircraft, seen here on arrival and spotting its original paint scheme with white markings. Before landing, it did a few spectacular low flypasts to the delight of the waiting photographers. The wooded background forms a part of the composition of the picture and it helps to act as a reference level. To photograph relatively large aircraft like this SR-71A, you need a medium zoom or a medium telephoto lens and to use a fast shutter speed.

Lockheed SR-71A 17975 of 9 SRW (USAF)

RAF Alconbury Air Tatoo '84 July 1984
(Pentax MEF 300mm f11 1/500 Fujicolor HR100)

The most interesting aircraft in the flying display at this air show is undoubtedly this SR-71A Blackbird which gave a very impressive performance to the great delight of the watching crowds. In this slow flypast, it banked slightly towards the crowd-line with the re-heat functioning on one engine only. The aircraft despite its new low-visibility paint scheme, is still one of the most photogenic aircraft you can find. Any picture taken from any angle should look very impressive.

McDonnell Douglas RF-4C Phantom 80583/AR of 10 TRW (USAF)

RAF Alconbury Air Tatoo '84 July 1984
(Pentax MX 400mm f8 1/1000 Fujicolor HR100)

A high speed, low-level tactical reconnaissance version of the F-4 Phantom family, this RF-4C is pictured here climbing gently away after its take-off run. This low-angle, take-off shot or it could easily be a simulated air-to-air shot, shows both its afterburners fully lit up against a bright blue sky. This photograph was taken about half-way along the runway, which is usually the lift-off point for most aircraft.

Dassault-Breguet Etendard IVP No.120 of 16F Aeronavale (Fr. Navy)

RAF St. Mawgan International Air Day August 1984
(Pentax MEF 300mm f8+½ 1/500 Fujicolor HR100)

Spotting a new two-tone camouflage scheme, this Etendard IVP photo-reconnaissance aircraft of the Aeronavale is the 'star' participant at the a r show. Sometimes, at the end of the flying display, some of the static aircraft may be towed out and prepared to fly back to their home bases. So by staying late, one may frequently get the chance for a take-off shot of an aircraft like this Etendard IVP, which has previously been displayed only statically.

Dassault-Breguet Mirage VBR BR-03 of 42 Sqn. (Bel.AF)

A reconnaissance version of the Mirage V fighter-bomber aircraft is this Mirage VBR of the Belgian Air Force, one is seen here on finals to participate in the IAT '83. This side-on view of the aircraft at almost tree-top level, was taken with a medium zoom lens which is generally suitable for taking shots of landing aircraft of all sizes except the smallest ones. Using the panning technique, it resulted in a crisp image of the aircraft set against a blurred wooded background, thus creating an impression of motion in the picture. The overcast conditions help to provide better details on the subject than if it was taken on a sunny day.

RAF Greenham Common IAT '83 July 1983
(Pentax ME Super 80-200mm f11 1/250 Fujicolor HR100)

Boeing T-43A 11404 of 323 FTW (USAF)

RAF Mildenhall Air Fete '81 May 1981
(Pentax ME Super 80-200mm f11 1/250 Kodacolor II)

Making its public debut at an air show in the UK is this T-43A navigator trainer aircraft. Seen here taxiing out for a training sortie after having arrived here to participate in the air show. To get good taxiing shots, you need to be in the right spot, which is near the taxiway at the downwind end of the runway. All taxiing aircraft usually stop here briefly before take-off, thus giving adequate time to focus or change lenses to cope with different sized aircraft. The same spot is also ideal for taking landing shots provided the light is right.

British Aerospace (BAC) Jet Provost T.5A XW437/39 of CFS (RAF)

RAF Greenham Common IAT '76 June 1976
(Pentax SPII 85-210mm f11 1/125 Kodacolor II)

This beautiful picture of a Jet Provost T.5A trainer aircraft doing a low-level, high speed flypast, was taken by using accurate panning and a medium fast shutter speed. It clearly shows a sharp image of the aircraft, subdues distracting background detail by blurring it and conveys a feeling of fast motion associated with an aircraft in flight. The subject matter only forms a small part in the overall composition of the picture.

Bell 212 No.210 of 120 Sqn. (R. of Sin.AF)

Republic of Singapore AF Air Display at Changi AFB June 1977
(Pentax SPII 85-210mm f8 1/1000 Kodacolor II)

This Bell 212 search and rescue helicopter from No.120 Sqn., was photographed in action at the Republic of Singapore Air Force Air Display at Changi AFB. It was doing a typical search and rescue demonstration before the crowds. The winchman can be seen just about to be lowered down to the ground. The motion of its twin rotor blades seems to be 'frozen' still by the use of a fast shutter speed, thus giving it a most unrealistic impression. A slower shutter speed of 1/250 sec. or even 1/125 sec. should have been used instead.

Boeing-Vertol HH-46A Sea Knight 151939/14 of PMTC (US Navy)

NAS Point Mugu Open House, USA October 1983
(Pentax MX 400mm f8 1/1000 Fujicolor HR100)

One of the local-based search and rescue helicopters is this HH-46A Sea Knight, seen here doing a slow flypast just before the main flying display starts. Caught unaware of its sudden appearance, a fast shutter speed was wrongly used for this shot. Sometimes, one may forget about changing shutter speed when photographing aircraft and then shortly followed by helicopters or vice versa.

The 'Blue Angels'—A-4F Skyhawks

The US Navy's aerobatic display team the 'Blue Angels', flying six A-4F Skyhawks, is world famous for its very tight formation display as you can see in this photo. Beginning its flying display in a spectacular way with this tight knife-edge formation flypast along the crowd-line. This view shows well the compression of perspective which is the hallmark of a 400mm telephoto lens. In addition, by using a motor-drive, several successive shots of this flypast resulted in a series of slightly different positions of the formation. This illustrates clearly the usefulness of a motor-drive in action photography.

NAS Point Mugu Open House, USA October 1983
(Pentax MX 400mm f8 1/1000 Fujicolor HR100)

The 'Blue Angels'—A-4F Skyhawks

NAS Point Mugu Open House, USA October 1983
(Pentax MX 400mm f8 1/1000 Fujicolor HR100)

Pictured in action here is a formation of 4 A-4F Skyhawks of the 'Blue Angels' which consists of 2 aircraft flying upright and 2 inverted. This tight formation makes a spectacular picture by itself. When photographing any aerobatic display team in action and to ensure all the aircraft are in focus, one should choose a small aperture whenever possible. In addition, the tightness of a formation can vary widely, so the best lens to use is a medium zoom with its variable focal lengths.

The 'Thunderbirds'—F-16A Fighting Falcons

Edwards AFB Open House, USA October 1983
(Pentax ME Super 80-200mm f16 1/250 Fujicolor HR100)

The immaculate line-up of 6 F-16As of the USAF's aerobatic display team, the 'Thunderbirds', seen here getting ready to taxi out. Most line-ups of aerobatic display teams are often not possible to photograph as they are usually parked well away from the crowd-line. Often there are all kinds of obstructions and clutter around these aircraft. As a result, a clean, uncluttered view is almost impossible to achieve. To keep both near and far details in focus, a small aperture should be used if possible when photographing any line-up of aircraft.

The 'Thunderbirds' — F-16A Fighting Falcons

A spectacular shot of a formation take-off by the 'Thunderbirds' display team to start its display. This photo shows the powerful engines of the F-16As with their afterburners fully lit and creating a shimmering haze over the runway. Sometimes, a more interesting and effective picture can be achieved by the careful selective enlargement of the negative or transparency.

RAF Upper Heyford Open Day June 1984
(Pentax MX 400mm f8 1/1000 Fujicolor HR100)

The 'Thunderbirds'—F-16A Fighting Falcons

At its 1984 European debut venue at RAF Upper Heyford, the 'Thunderbirds' display team was photographed here against an unusually blue sky. Flying in a perfect diamond formation, the four aircraft were banking towards the crowd-line when this shot was taken. A 400mm telephoto is the most suitable lens for this kind of shot as its length represents the limit of what can be comfortably hand-held. A good piece of advice during any flying display is always be alert for any surprise manoeuvre.

RAF Upper Heyford Open Day June 1984
(Pentax MX 400mm f8 1/1000 Fujicolor HR100)

The 'Thunderbirds'—F-16A Fighting Falcons

The 'Thunderbirds' are pictured here in action as they were performing a diamond formation pass with all gear down. The USAF's aerobatic display team with its colourful F-16A Fighting Falcons make a spectacular picture just by the formation itself. A perfect formation set against a perfect blue sky and when carefully composed should produce a good, spectacular action photo.

RAF Upper Heyford Open Day June 1984
(Pentax ME Super 80-200mm f16 1/250 Fujicolor HR100)

The 'Red Arrows'—Hawk T.1s

The RAF's aerobatic display team the 'Red Arrows' is pictured here as it swings down to complete a loop in a diamond formation. Sometimes, formation shots of aerobatic display teams can easily look dull and uninteresting unless they are carefully composed and use is made of the vapour trails as part of the composition. This photo of the 'Red Arrows' with its smoke trails, conveys a feeling of motion to a still picture, particularly when they show changes of direction. The perfect blue afternoon sky helps to enhance the picture considerably.

RAF Fairford Open Day July 1984
(Pentax MX 400mm f8 1/1000 Fujicolour HR100)

The 'Red Arrows'—Hawk T.1s

RAF Fairford Open Day July 1984
(Pentax MX 400mm f8 1/1000 Fujicolor HR100)

Making its dramatic break at the end of its display, the 'Red Arrows' performs this spectacular 'parasol break' when all nine Hawk T.1 aircraft dispersed into all directions. Knowing the usual routine manoeuvers in a 'Red Arrows' display certainly helps the photographer to anticipate its next move and therefore be ready with the camera. For photographing any aerobatic display team which uses smoke trails, the nature of the sky backdrop affects the quality of the picture. Sometimes, white smoke trails may not show up well against an overcast or cloudy sky.

The 'Patrouille de France'—Alpha Jet Es

Making one of its rare appearances in the UK is the French Air Force's aerobatic display team the 'Patrouille de France', photographed here performing a smoke-on pass before the crowds. These eight brightly painted Alpha Jet E aircraft flying in an immaculate formation, makes a spectacular picture, just by the formation itself.

RAF Greenham Common IAT '83 July 1983
(Pentax ME Super 80-200mm f11 1/250 Fujicolor HR100)

The addition of colourful smoke trails, make it even more spectacular. Whenever possible, choose a small aperture in order to ensure all the aircraft in the formation are within the depth of field.

Boeing 747 No.905 (NASA)

Stansted Airport June 1983
(Pentax ME Super 80-200mm f8+½ 1/250 Fujicolor HR100)

The arrival of the NASA Boeing 747 aircraft with the US Space Shuttle 'Enterprise' on its back, to Stansted Airport was undoubtedly the aviation event of 1983 in the UK. It literally brought the traffic around the airport to a standstill. Finding a good spot in the vicinity of the landing approach was not easy due mainly to overcrowding, inaccessible areas and trees. Not an ideal day for photography, as it was dull and cloudy when the aircraft appeared over the airport.

Curtiss P-40E Kittyhawk N94466

RAF Fairford Open Day July 1984
(Pentax MX 400mm f8 1/1000 Fujicolor HR100)

A newcomer to the air show circuit in the UK is this shark-mouthed P-40E Kittyhawk aircraft, sporting a colourful desert camouflage scheme. This long telephoto view was taken during a low flypast as it was banking towards the crowd-line. At this close-up view even the faces in the cockpit can be just recognisable. It also shows details of the aircraft not noticeable from other angles.

US Space Shuttle 'Enterprise' (NASA)

Edwards AFB Open House October 1983
(Pentax MEF 35-105mm f16 1/250 Fujicolor HR100)

The US Space Shuttle 'Enterprise' was the 'star' item in the static display and therefore, it did attract many onlookers around it for most of the day. In this case, a good uncluttered shot will be difficult to get. In general, if you want to photograph the static display aircraft, you should always arrive early at the air show and with a little patience, you should be able to get relatively uncluttered shots. A wide angle or a short zoom lens is essential for any static display photography.

British Aerospace Concorde G-BOAE (British Airways)

RAF Fairford Open Day July 1984
(Pentax ME Super 80-200mm f11+½ 1/250 Fujicolor HR100)

A Concorde supersonic airliner is a highly photogenic subject itself and it is always a favourite among photographers as well as spectators. The aesthetic lines of a Concorde look good from any angle. During this display, it did a few spectacular flypasts including touch and go, and with reheats on all its four engines as can be seen in this photo. On the whole, this must be the most impressive display yet by a Concorde in any air show.

De Havilland Sea Vixen D.3 XP924 of Flight Refuelling Ltd.

RNAS Yeovilton International Air Day August 1982
(Pentax ME Super 80-200mm f11 1/250 Kodacolor II)

This dramatic and perfectly timed shot of a rather colourful Sea Vixen D.3 aircraft from Aberporth, shows the aircraft kicking up dust just as its wheels touched the runway. The dust clouds, the sharp image of the aircraft and the blurred background, all help to convey a feeling of motion to an otherwise still picture. Getting good action shots from the ground is often the case of knowing the right spot to be at and the right moment to release the shutter.

Supermarine Spitfire P.R.19 PM631 of B of BMF

RAF Upper Heyford Open Day June 1983
(Pentax MX 400mm f8 1/1000 Fujicolor HR100)

The Battle of Britain Memorial Flight's Spitfire P.R.19, the world's most famous fighter plane, is pictured here sporting new markings including 'invasion-type' stripes. This Spitfire was doing a low flypast with its wings slightly dipped towards the crowd-line. Any low-flying aircraft should make a spectacular picture if the ground can be included to act as a reference level. A Spitfire in flight is a highly photogenic subject and it should make an impressive picture if it can be photographed at close quarters or with the help of a long telephoto lens.

Antonov An-72 'Coaler' CCCP 72000 (Aeroflot)

Farnborough International Air Show '84 September 1984
(Pentax MX 1000mm f11 1/500 Fujicolor HR400)

Taken on the Press day, this spectacular view of the Russian STOL airliner An-72 'Coaler', shows it banking steeply for a landing approach. This photo was actually taken with a 1000mm f11 mirror lens and hand-held at 1/500 sec. Normally for such a heavy and big lens, it is better to fix it on a tripod or a monopod. But unfortunately, it may be difficult to use for photographing fast jets in flight or in any crowded situation like the crowd-line in an air show. As it is a slow lens, focussing becomes more critical and also don't forget to use fast films of 200 ASA or 400 ASA as well.